Your Guide to Amazon Prime
&
Amazon Echo

Part 1: Amazon Echo:
*Easy-to-Use Guide for
Amazon Echo, Dot, and Tap*

Part 2: Amazon Prime:

*How to Make the Most Out of
the Many Benefits of Amazon
Prime Membership*

Amazon Echo

Easy-to-Use Guide for Amazon Echo, Dot, and Tap

Table of Contents

Introduction:

I want to thank you and congratulate you for downloading *Amazon Echo: Easy-to-Use Guide for Amazon Echo, Dot, and Tap.*

This book contains proven steps and strategies on how to most efficiently use your new Alexa powered Amazon device. There is no greater proof that we are living in a time of the future than with how incredibly powerful digital assistants have become. Amazon's Alexa digital assistant is currently the market leader with an incredible understanding of natural human speech and holds the lead in a number of connected third-party apps and services. Alexa puts you in better control of your home and the features within.

I want to give you the information you need to get the most out of your Alexa powered device. Whether you're a tech wizard or a computer novice, this book offers useful tips and information on how to make sure you are using Alexa to her utmost potential.

Here's an inescapable fact: Amazon's Alexa is constantly being updated with new features and finding integration with the latest in third-party services. To stay current on Alexa and all the amazing things she can do you will need this book. There are tons of features that hiding just under the surface of your Amazon Echo powered device.

If you do not learn about all of the amazing features that Amazon's Alexa brings to the digital assistant marketplace, then you will be wasting a great deal of your brand new device's potential. There is an opportunity here to have your house set up exactly as you always pictured it – a futuristic home where information and control are just a voice command away. You took a leap of faith by purchasing an Echo powered device; now it's time to see the fruit of your purchase and learn about all of the truly incredible things Alexa can do for you.

It's time for you to jump start your home into the 21st century with the latest in digital technology. Using the power of the cloud and the tips in this book, Alexa will become a gateway to a better future with more control over your home, access to information at your fingertip, and entertainment that can be enjoyed for the entire household. Come and join me as you learn about the simple tricks and the mind-bending features that Alexa holds!

Chapter 1: Basics of the Echo, Tap, and Dot

No matter the device that you purchase from Amazon, whether it's the Echo, Tap or Dot, you will be receiving the world's most advanced digital assistant. Alexa is Amazon's answer to Microsoft's Cortana and Apple's Siri – she is a digital assistant that is miles ahead of the competition and has a much greater set of core abilities.

Alexa's greatest strengths come in her ability to network with your home's lighting, thermostat, and more. The difference between the Echo, Dot, and Tap lie in how they encase Alexa and how they gate access to her services.

Digital assistants are nothing new in the tech world. You are probably most familiar with Apple's Siri that first debuted on the iPhone 4S in 2011 and has grown more capable ever since.

Still, the digital assistant has not brought about the great change that was promised in advertising campaigns and leaders in the tech world. Siri has her uses, but overall the digital assistant is not effective enough to be used every day.

A lot of this has to do with just *how* we access assistants like Siri and Cortana. For both assistants, the input lies on your phone. We carry our phones everywhere we go but reaching into your pocket to verbally command your phone to do something that you can just as quickly do in a few button presses simply not practical; it is not solving an existing problem.

This is where Alexa truly shines; not only does Alexa offer better integration with apps and services, but she is fundamentally more useful in that she is connected to your home. Alexa will never need to rest in your pocket, and you will never need to fish her out of your bag.

Once Alexa has been properly setup on any supported Echo device (Echo, Tap, Dot), she can register a user's commands from a great distance. The utility of requesting information at a moment's notice, without having to reach for your phone, cannot be understated.

If you have been unimpressed with digital assistants before, think about how cumbersome their use was in that you had to be constantly reaching for your phone.

Now imagine simply speaking to your home and being able to get consistently the information you were seeking – this is the future that Alexa brings to your household. Your first task in integrating Alexa into your life is choosing how you will house your new assistant.

Alexa's Home In The Cloud

Alexa does not live inside of the Tap, Echo, or Dot, but is rather stored in the cloud. This means that Alexa can process voice requests with far greater precision due to the increase in power she is able to draw from cloud computing. As you make requests to Alexa, the information is being transmitted to Amazon and Amazon's computers can crunch the data much faster than any personal computer can.

This does mean that you will need a steady internet connection to use Alexa effectively, but in turn, you gain a massive increase in computing power and remove the fear of needing to upgrade Alexa in the future. Alexa will constantly improve as she is enhanced on Amazon's servers and there is no purchase necessary to access these enhancements.

The choice you have to make is what type of hardware you want to hold Alexa. The hardware will determine the size that Alexa takes up in your home, the power draw she uses, and the clarity of the audio she emits and how well she can hear your own voice.

Currently, Amazon offers three choices for consumers all coming at various price points; there is something for every shopper.

Amazon Echo

The Amazon Echo is the marquee Echo device that Amazon has been selling for the longest amount of time.

This product comes in at $179.99 and is the best product for consumers that want high-quality audio and the best audio pickup for taking requests from all over your home.

The Echo has a large cylindrical form factor with a speaker that wraps 360 degrees around the entire body of the device.

There are no displays on the device, and everything is handled with your voice. The only exception to this is the initial setup which is handled through your iOS or Android device.

Picture courtesy of Amazon.com

The Echo is the most expensive Alexa device for your home, but it is also comes packed with the best quality speakers and recording pickups. If you are looking for a device for your living room or kitchen, this is probably what you are going to want to buy.

The price is a little bit steep, but unlike tablets and Amazon's other devices like the Kindle, the core of the Echo is entirely software based and updates will come for years and will always be free.

The main upgrades that will come to the Echo in future hardware revisions will be more impressive recorders and better speakers, but as far as the tech world is concerned, audio hardware will not have the massive improvements that other tech devices receive after only a few years.

Echo Dot

The Amazon Dot, commonly referred to as the Echo Dot, is a smaller more compact version of its larger brother. The Dot has a fantastically slim form factor that can fit on just about anywhere. When this product initially came out, there was actually quite a bit of confusion as to how it fit into the entire Echo ecosystem. Due to some slight brand confusion, it was once thought that a regular Amazon Echo was required to use the Echo Dot – this is not true, however, and the Echo Dot can be used entirely independently from the larger Amazon Echo.

Picture courtesy of
BussinessInsider.com

The Echo Dot is the most compact Amazon device featuring Alexa but still requires a standard power outlet and is for use strictly inside the home. The small form factor means a less powerful speaker and receiver, but don't be fooled; the Dot can still be heard from a great distance and can pick up your voice from across a large room.

Packing the same power as the larger Echo, the main difference in the Dot comes in its philosophy of use.

If the larger Echo was designed for use in one large room, then the Echo Dot was designed to be placed in multiple rooms all across your house. The lower price point of $89.99 makes the Echo Dot more appealing if you plan on filling your home with multiple Echo devices, but know that each device functions independently from one another.

This means that while each Echo might be connected to the same services throughout your home, having two Echo Dots next to each and asking Alexa a question will be met with the same answer coming from two different devices. An ideal use of the Echo Dot is placing them in rooms where your voice won't be picked up on the other device.

Currently, the Echo Dot is the most popular Alexa supported device. The price point is appealing to a wide variety of consumers, and the form factor fits in nicely with just about any room in the house.

The Echo Dot could originally only be purchased if you already had an Amazon Echo or if you knew someone that had one. As the device starts to come back in stock, it's possible orders made through other Echo devices will be given priority, so if you are desperate for an Echo Dot you may want to try asking your friend's Alexa to order one.

It will come through your friend's account, but this is currently the fastest way of securing an Echo Dot. To place an order, simply ask Alexa to "Order an Echo Dot."

Amazon Tap

The Amazon Tap is the second iteration of Echo devices and is designed as an Alexa on the go. It's best to think about the Amazon Tap as a Bluetooth speaker that happens to come with Alexa as a digital assistant.

While this means that you can use the Amazon Tap outside of the home, the device also has significantly lower audio quality than the other Amazon Echo devices and is less feature rich in hardware. To gain access to Alexa, you must *tap* the device and cannot merely call out to Alexa. This makes the way that you interact with the Tap much more in line with how most users use Siri or Cortana.

Picture courtesy of Wired.com

The Amazon Tap comes in at $130 but is frequently discounted and sold for as little as $110. The device has all of the trappings of its two siblings, but its initial design as a Bluetooth speaker is quite apparent.

It seems as though the designers were creating a portable speaker device for Amazon and the Alexa features were added towards the end of development. This is made evident by how the user is forced to *tap* the device to access Alexa.

The positives of the Amazon Tap are that it is fully wireless and can run up to nine hours on battery power. This puts the device in line with other Bluetooth speakers regarding battery life, but its price point is on the more expensive side for these types of devices.

The main purpose of the Tap is to amplify audio coming out of your smartphone, and it does this to decent success. The audio quality is good, but it isn't great. If you are looking for a dedicated Bluetooth speaker there are better and cheaper devices, and as far as Alexa powered devices go the other choices offer potentially better usability due to voice controls.

This is, however, the one Echo device that works on the go. If Alexa becomes a major part of your life, then it could be worthwhile bringing the Amazon Tap with you as you travel.

Chapter 2: Which Device Is Right For You?

There are several different price points for Echo devices and depending on what you are seeking; there is going to be an appropriate choice just for you. You must remember that the main selling point of all Echo devices is the Alexa digital assistant, and each Echo device has the same level of performance when it comes to tasks that Alexa will handle.

Since Alexa's computations are done on a remote server, the speed of responses will largely be the same across devices, with major changes in variability coming from the quality of your internet connection. In terms of bandwidth however Alexa is quite light on resources, and you shouldn't have any problems unless you are using an ADSL or satellite connection.

The main differentiator across Echo devices is then the form factor and quality of the speakers and recording devices on each product, as well as the price of each product. Each device has their own pros and cons but in essence, you are receiving the same experience regardless of the product you choose. Keep this in mind as you shop and you should be able to find a device that fits your needs and works within your budget.

Amazon Echo

At $179.99 the Amazon Echo is the most expensive in the Echo line of devices, but it is also the most feature rich. Coming packed with the most powerful speaker system of the three and the best range on its built-in recorder, the Echo is great for family rooms and parts of the house where you are likely to get a lot of foot traffic.

This model is great for playing music at parties or answering simple conversion question in a kitchen. Its place in larger rooms where the whole family spends time makes it also able to adapt to each member of the family, getting more familiar with each voice and being able to pinpoint what a family member is saying, even if they have a heavy accent.

The cost and size of this device are its main detractors, and if you are looking for an Echo device for your bedroom, there are better choices. Also while the speaker quality is quite good, audiophiles will likely want to set up external speakers to get the best quality audio.

Serving the purpose of large family rooms, the pickup of the recording device on the original Echo is quite strong, and while you can disable the recorder entirely, if you are worried about surveillance or setting Alexa off accidently, this model will have the greatest listening range of the three.

Lastly, if a new hardware revision for any Echo device is going to arrive soon, it will first arrive for this model. While the Echo is still very new, and if you are interested in one I do think you should pick one up now, the original Echo is the oldest device, and so it will likely see the first hardware revision. Again since Alexa is powered by the cloud, this does not mean a faster device necessarily, but you can probably expect slightly better speakers and a more capable microphone, as well as a possible price cut if manufacturing gets cheaper.

Echo Dot

Personally, this is my favorite Echo Device – there are pieces of hardware that you hold that really make you feel like you are in the future. The last time I experienced this feeling prior to the Echo Dot was with the original iPhone. The power of Alexa rests in the cloud, and the Echo Dot uses this to its advantage by being the smallest Echo device available. It fits great on any table, and its elegant design makes it easy on the eyes.

The recorder and speakers on the device, while not as powerful as the full-sized Echo, are quite good and have excellent range in small to medium sized rooms. The price point is also the most affordable at $89.99, giving you an incentive to add more to your home if you find that you would like to use Alexa in different parts of your house. The feature set is exactly the same as the other Echo devices, and Alexa can connect to your home and manage all of the same systems.

As the Echo Dot originally rolled out there was quite a bit of confusion as to how it functions with other Echo products in your home. This is largely due to how orders were first placed for the Echo Dot.

Originally orders could only be placed through the first Amazon Echo, and so the Dot was thought of as a companion device. It was stated in Chapter One, but it's important to note that the Echo Dot is a stand alone device, and you do not need any other Echo products to get all of its functionality.

The main negative to the Echo Dot is it is currently impossible to find. Alexa and the Amazon Echo are great ideas, but the original price point was a little bit too much for consumers that were on the edge.

The Echo Dot seems to have found the right price point to allure a great number of consumers, but unfortunately, the manufacturing and supply chain on parts has left many of consumers without any way of ordering the product.

If you are interested in the Echo Dot, be on the lookout for when Amazon starts shipping them again. It's possible that Amazon will lock orders behind a Prime membership, as they have done with other Echo devices in the past, but know that Amazon Prime offers several apps that will heighten your experience with any Echo device.

While it is doubtful that when orders for the Dot open up again, they will only be taken on other Echo devices, this is something to keep in mind, and you may want to track down a friend that already has an Echo. When the Echo Dot becomes available ordering a Dot through your friend's Echo might be the bet way to ensure receiving the product.

Amazon Tap

The Amazon Tap is an overall difficult product to recommend. It seems like a device that was changed several times through development, and the overall product is less than impressive.

If you are looking for an Alexa powered device that you can take with you outside of the home, then the Amazon Tap is the best option. Running on battery power, the Tap can provide nine hours of audio and cloud integration ensures the Alexa is just as fast on the Tap as it is on any other Echo product. **The drawbacks** of the device, however, might be a little bit too much to justify a purchase and the relatively heavy price tag it carries.

At $130 the Amazon Tap is neither a great Bluetooth speaker nor the best Alexa powered device. Standing somewhere in the middle between these two devices the Tap comes with a lot of drawbacks that hampers the whole experience. Communication with Alexa is not done through voice communication but by hitting a button on the device and so it will have to be close by to use the digital assistant.

The battery life at nine hours might seem impressive, but as far as Bluetooth speakers go, the audio quality does not justify the nine hours of battery draw. The audio is murky in the best of conditions and some genres of music can sounds flat out bad through its low voltage speakers.

On the bright side, the microphone is quite good at picking up your voice after you've *tapped* the device. The price point of $130 might seem a little bit steep, but it is currently the cheapest Echo device that can easily be found.

I wouldn't expect Amazon to continue the Tap line of products in the future. In a lot of ways, this seems like a fluke product and the Tap name is so ingrained with Alexa being locked behind a button that chances of a follow-up under the same branding are slim.

This does mean you should not buy the Tap if the feature set is exactly what you want, but you should probably purchase one now before production stops. In terms of software and firmware updates Amazon has stated that they will stand behind the Tap. However it seems likely that updates for the Tap will be discontinued before other more popular Echo products.

Chapter 3: Your New Digital Assistant (Basic Tasks)

You've chosen your Amazon Echo device, and you are ready to be acquainted with your new digital assistant, Alexa. Alexa is voice activated on the Amazon Dot and Amazon Echo – by simply using the key phrase "Alexa", the Echo will wake from its sleep and be ready for a wide variety of inputs.

These requests can range from simple tasks to complicated multi-step dialogues. A lot of the fun with Alexa comes from experimentation and seeing just how natural she can act. Don't be afraid to try commands even if they aren't listed in this book.

What I really want you to gain is understand how Alexa uses information and some of the great uses that she can have in your home. In this chapter I will simply be discussing Alexa as if she was connected to your home network and no third party applications were loaded. This is what Alexa can do out of the box and once your Echo device has been set up.

Setup

You'll notice that your Amazon Echo does not have a display. Setting up your device and your account information is handled on your iOS or Android device. Simply download the Alexa app from the App Store or Google Play store, plug in your Echo device, and look for the settings under your Alexa app. The app will control your Echo device and dictate which wireless network to connect to.

I know that you've probably connected devices to your wireless network before, and the Echo is largely the same, but there is one key difference you will want to take note of. Alexa does not need a lot of bandwidth or data to function as best she can, but she does need a very low latency connection with minimal packet loss. This might sound very technical, and that's OK – what we are trying to do here is make sure that Alex has the most *stable* connection, not necessarily the *fastest* connection.

If you are living in an apartment, I suggest using the 5 GHz band that Alexa supports as most routers now come with this as a standard feature. The 5 GHz frequency is above the frequency that most other devices use, and you will run into less interference.

If you are living in a home or if you are placing your Echo far away from your wireless access point, you'll want to use the 2.4 GHz band as this can be used from a further distance. Again, do not worry about the speed of Alexa butt rather just the consistently in her connection.

Privacy

Unless you are using the Amazon Tap, your Echo device Alexa will constantly be listening for her activation phrase. This does not mean that Alexa is processing your every word, but it does mean that she is constantly drawing power and on the lookout for her name. The moment Alexa hears "Alexa," she will begin to process your next sentence and seek to give you an answer. This is the main selling point of Alexa, but there may be times when you want to avoid Alexa from listening for her activation phrase, whether it be a business meeting or a romantic evening with a significant other.

To turn off Alexa's recorder simply hold down the noise cancellation button on the top of the Echo device. You will want to press this button until a red circle lights up on the top of the cylinder. You cannot disable this setting through your voice and will have to press the button again to enable Alexa.

Natural Language

Alexa is the first digital assistant that *actually* works. Siri and Cortana have functionality, but so many of their answers rely on the quality of the question. Alexa is much smarter than other digital assistants and is great at parsing natural language. You will always need the initial activation phrase to start Alexa, but after this feel free to speak naturally.

This includes following up questions as Alexa will remember the topic at hand and you will not need to define the subject matter again. If you are curious about "Who won the World Series in 1954?" Alexa would answer and any other query about World Series winners could be asked with "What about in 19xx?"

If you ever miss a response that Alexa provides, you can simply say "Alexa can you repeat that?" and she will default to giving you the answer to your last question. Experiment and try different ways of asking questions; the point here is you don't need to speak with Alexa as she is simply a Google search tool.

Uses In The Kitchen

It's best to think about Alexa as a guide to the internet. She can relay most pieces of information from recipes to sports scores, but she can also do many of the simple functions that you might use Google for.

A great use of Alexa is in her powerful conversion tools. If you find yourself in the kitchen and unsure of how many tablespoons of butter you need because the recipe measures the ingredient in cups, then simply ask Alexa to convert between cups and tablespoons. This can be done in specific amounts as well such as "3 cups to tablespoons".

Alexa can also be quite handy when a Google search can fix your recipe. If you've ever found yourself out of vanilla extract and preparing to wash yourself off before you sit down at a computer to look for a substitute, Alexa can help with that. Alexa is great at reading the information on results and for simple questions like these, she can inform you of a substitute without you needing to waste time washing your hands and going to your desktop.

Chapter Five will go more in depth on third party services, but Alexa has recently been upgraded to interact with the latest in smart refrigerators. Currently, these are limited to Samsung brand refrigerators, but features like meal recipe ideas based on the ingredients in your fridge are possible. The information that Alexa is drawing from is entirely from your refrigerator, and the quality of the recipes currently rests in the hands of Samsung.

Your Kids And Alexa

Perhaps I'm old-fashioned, but as a child, in elementary school, I remember going home and doing my homework at the kitchen table. I would constantly pester my mother by asking her spelling questions and history questions while she was working away at household chores.

If your child does homework in the same room that your Amazon Echo sits, you will want to introduce them to Alexa. Your children will have to use the same key phrase of "Alexa" before every question, but Alexa is great for all types of basic school questions.

For fun, you can also ask Alexa to provide you or your child with questions. If you ask Alexa for a "spelling bee word," she will ask you to spell a word and tell you if you are correct.

Alexa is prepared to handle questions ranging from math to spelling, to geography, and everything in-between. Having your child use Alexa gives them a tool to quickly and accurately get a response to every question no matter how big or small.

Alexa also has the great advantage of you being to hear your children's inquiries. If you moderate how much internet usage your child gets, this can be a great help. You'll know that their online searches are related to schoolwork because you will actually hear their requests.

Chapter 4: Music and Entertainment through Alexa

The power of Alexa comes in her ability to sync with different apps and services across a variety of media. By and far the single most useful media type is audio, and Alexa provides a great way to listen to audiobooks, podcasts, and music.

Alexa does not need a specific request to get started and will respond to a general query for music, or even a specific genre of music. Issuing the command "Alexa, play some classic rock" will create a playlist and start playing from any sources that hold music of this genre. Depending on when or if you started to collect digital music, how you listen and what apps you use is gong to be slightly different.

Listening To The Music You Own

Any music that you have purchased through Amazon will be stored on your prime account and can be easily accessed using Alexa. However, I have found that most of the music I listen to through Alexa is my own.

This means MP3s that I have gathered over the years and have uploaded to Amazon's music streaming service. Now if you are above a certain age of around forty or below a certain age of about twenty-five, then you are likely only using streaming services, but there are many of us in the middle that came of age to the internet during the time of Napster, Morpheus, and the CD ripping subculture. If any of this sounds familiar, then there is a good chance that you are sitting on several gigabytes of music.

For absolutely free, you can upload up to 250 of your own MP3s and play them back on any Amazon device, including all Amazon Echo products. If you are holding onto more songs, then a yearly fee of $24.99 is required to upload up to 250,000 songs.

This should be enough space to upload your entire collection, and remember now with these songs in the cloud they can be played back from any device and anywhere as long as you have an internet connection. It should be noted that this music can only be played back if the corresponding profile is signed into Alexa.

Switching User Accounts

For all of your digital purchases through Amazon, whether audiobooks or music, this will always be tied to your account and you will always have access to this content. It's likely that in your household you have multiple Amazon accounts and will need to set up multiple profiles on your Echo device.

To do this, you will want to open the Alexa app on your smartphone and go to "settings", "accounts", and then "add user account". Alexa is only able to playback content that has been purchased on the currently signed in profile. While this may sound complicated, switching profiles are quite easy, and the only time investment is setting up multiple accounts using the Alexa app.

Once you have setup your user profiles on Alexa, you'll find an easy time switching between profiles. Simply say "Alexa account" and Alexa will ask what user account you want to log into.

If you are unsure of the account that is currently logged in, simply ask "Alexa what account is currently logged in?" Remember that Alexa is great at natural language and that there are various phrases you can use to switch accounts, so you don't need to worry about providing a specific phrase for each request.

The Available Music Apps

Currently, the Amazon Echo supports a wide range of streaming services. The most notably absent service is iTunes, but this is to be expected with an Amazon device. If you are interested in having your purchases on iTunes play through Alexa, you can use a workaround and upload your MP3s to Amazon's music store – for more information see *Listening To The Music You Own.*

The available services are listed below. Each service can be added to the Echo by opening the Alexa app on your smartphone and adding individual music apps.

- Amazon Music
- Prime Music
- Spotify Premium
- Pandora
- TuneIn
- iHeartRadio

- Audible

It is on your smartphone that you will always sign into music services. You should note that currently, music services are on an account level, so if you pay for a Spotify premium subscription, you will have to be signed into the corresponding Amazon account where you linked your Spotify information.

Switching profiles will leave you without access to the Spotify account. It has been a long requested feature that music services not be tied to accounts, and this feature will likely be included in a software update.

Picture courtesy of Cnet.com

Making a Purchase with Your Voice

If you are heavily involved in the Amazon eco system, making a purchase through your Echo can be a fast way to get what you need with a simple voice command.

I have found that most purchases I make through my Echo are audiobooks, songs, and albums, but you can also purchase other items and even reorder past orders all through Alexa. To allow voice purchasing go into "settings," "accounts," "authorize voice purchases" and then follow the instructions on your Alexa app through your smartphone.

Alexa will make sure that she can recognize your voice, so accidental purchases don't happen. This has saved me quite a few times when my kids attempt to order Minecraft music through our Echo.

Chapter 5: Controlling Your Home

Amazon Echo devices are constantly evolving how they interact with your home. Just this year a partnership was announced with the new line of Samsung refrigerators, and when set up, Alexa can let you know about every item in your fridge. She will even give you recipes based on what you have in stock or recommend purchases for your next outing to the supermarket.

As it currently stands, however, there are many ways to integrate Alexa into your home, offering you more control that can be accessed with simple voice commands.

Lighting

The best way to control atmospheric lighting in your home is through Phillip's Hue products and their integration with Alexa. After installing the lighting throughout your home, the lights will communicate via Bluetooth or through your wifi network (depending on the version of lights you buy).

Using the Philip's Hue application on your phone to set different light profiles, you can then activate a profile using Alexa. This is a great way to bring your home into the 21st century with not only voice-activated lights but with subtle changes to lighting that can alter the mood of any room in your house.

Picture courtesy of ylighting.com

This feature works with all Echo devices and can control lights that are not in the same room as the Echo device you are using. You may want to keep this in mind if you have children as they have a habit of using some of these more advanced features to play pranks. If it ever becomes a problem you can simply go into user accounts and make it so that light commands only work when controlled with certain voices.

You can program you and your significant other's voices so that only you have access. Note that in this scenario guests would not be able to control the lighting. It is expected that in an upcoming patch you will simply be able to block certain voices and allow all others, however at the time of this book this feature is still absent, so be mindful whom you want to lock out of control.

There are alternatives to Philip's Hue products, and these are being added all the time. I have a friend that has his entire home wired using Insteon products for the thermostat, lighting, and ceiling fan control. Alexa will work with each of these products and be able to control them independently.

While the software from Philips and Insteon is absolutely stellar, you will want to look into how each individual product works before making a purchase. Also less known brands do not necessary mean worse quality, but it does almost certainly mean less support in the future – this is not at the feet of Amazon but rather the company that updates the software for their products.

Alexa will always work with a product in the same way, but unless a company updates their profiles for Alexa, new functionally may not cross over in future updates.

Outlets

A much more cost efficient way to control the lighting in your house, or any electronic system, is through Belkin's WeMo product line. A WeMo simply plugs into your existing outlet and acts as a switch that is controlled over wifi. By going into the settings for Alexa, you can add this third party service. The main programming is done using the WeMo app, and key phrases are then set up on Alexa.

I currently use this system in my home to control the lighting in my den and dining room and to turn on and off my entertainment center. I found the voice controls for third party apps do not work as well with natural langue so you'll want to be careful what keywords you program.

For my wife and I, we had to program both "light group three" and "light three" into the accepted keywords to get both to register. You can have phrases for the same function, so don't worry about overlapping commands. You'll just want to make sure that you have programmed each keyword that you think you will use.

In terms of the cost, I found WeMo to be the best value for controlling nonspecific functions throughout our home. The average WeMo will run you $40, but sales are fairly frequent, and I was able to buy several at around $30 each. While I only use the WeMo to control the lighting and entertainment system in my house, there is no technical reason it cannot be used to control anything that plugs into an outlet. Some ideas for potential uses is controlling outside patio lighting, turning on and off a pool heater, or managing energy expenses if you use an in-window air conditioning unit.

Thermostat

There are quite a few thermostats that work with Alexa and they mostly all function the same way. While Alexa adds a new way to interact with your thermostat it does not replace its basic functionality, so if there is a feature that doesn't exist on your thermostat then do not expect Alexa to control that aspect.

For example, some of the more budget thermostats do not offer wattage controls where a thermostat will modify the temperature based on how much power you want to consume. If this feature is not built into the thermostat itself, then it will not work with Alexa.

There are only three brands of thermostat that I would recommend: Sensi, Insteon, and Nest. Sensi and Insteon are both affordable and a great value at around $100, but lack some of the learning features of the more expensive Nest brand at $250.

If you are concerned about power usage, then Nest is the brand to go with as their learning software is currently the best on the market and has been shown to greatly reduce energy costs.

Alexa will work the same way with all of these systems and commands to Alexa will simply relay to the app and then to the thermostat.

Chapter 6: Personal Trainer, Alarm Clock, and More

How you use the Alexa is going to be dependent very much on the needs you have in your home. I do suggest that you try and use Alexa in a variety of situations to see what works best for you. Every month new product integration is being added to Alexa – Amazon has taken to calling these features "skills." I use the following features nearly every single day, and without fail they make me feel like I am living in the future. Try these features and you too might fall in love with how easy Alexa can make certain tasks

Car Services

Both Uber and Lyft are supported on Alexa. By simply asking "Alexa can you get me an Uber/Lyft?", One will arrive at your door in just a few minutes. I love this feature and have found it much easier than reaching for my phone and using either app. You will need to go into the settings of your Echo using the Alexa app and add a device location, so drivers know where to pick you up. As you request a driver, Alexa will inform you of how far away the driver is and at what time you can expect the driver to arrive.

Exercise Routine

If you ask Alexa for an exercise routine, she will provide an intense seven-minute workout. This is a free third party skill that can be added by simply requesting a workout. Most skills such as these simply need a keyword, and they will be downloaded and installed on your Echo device instantly. The workout routine has already seen several updates and will provide you with a variety of different workouts

Alarm Clock and Calendar

It's quite a simple feature, but Alexa's alarm clock is invaluable. Asking Alexa to set an alarm for five minutes is a feature I use every night as I cook. The calendar function is also quite impressive as Alexa can interpret two dates and give the number of days in-between.

If you ask Alexa "How many days are between now and January 1st?" she will be able to interpret that you mean January of next year and be able to calculate the number of days instantly.

I use this feature when I quickly need to know how many weeks are before a certain date. Alexa comes pre-programmed with dates for Holidays as well, so you can try asking for the number of days until Christmas, and she will provide the appropriate response.

Trivia and Easter Eggs

The programmers at Amazon have equipped Alexa with an absolute trove of trivia and a ton of Eas *Picture courtesy of Wareable.com* display here, but I suggest you try asking Alexa all sort of trivia questions. Most answers are pre-programmed, but she is also able to produce an answer using Google search results.

As for Easter Eggs, Alexa is best used when asked for information about famous robots. If you ask her about Skynet or the Hal 9000, she will certainly have something to say. Unlike Siri, there are thousands of Easter Eggs hidden away in Alexa's programming.

I love to ask Alexa all types of questions just to see if she has a funny response or a clever answer. When your new Echo device arrives, try saying "Alexa, I am your father" – not only will she have a great quip, but she has dozens of responses that are all relevant and funny.

Conclusion:

Thank you again for downloading *Amazon Echo: Easy-to-Use Guide for Amazon Echo, Dot, and Tap.*

I hope this book was able to help you select the Echo device that is right for you and to get you acquainted with all of the incredible things Alexa is capable of. Regardless of the Echo device that you decided on, the real achievement is in Alexa and how capable of a digital assistant she is.

I hope that she will be as impactful on your life as she has been on mine. So many technologies promise a glimpse of the future, but ever since I connected my home to Alexa, I feel like that promise has finally been met.

The next step is to setup your Amazon Echo device and to start experimenting with Alexa. Make sure to connect Alexa to all of your favorite streaming services and to be constantly on the lookout for new skills. Your Echo device is one that will grow better over time so make sure stay up to date with all of the amazing things Alexa can do.

Finally, if you enjoyed this book, please take the time to share your thoughts and post a review on Amazon. It'd be greatly appreciated!

Thank you and good luck!

Amazon Prime:

How to Make the Most Out of the Many Benefits of Amazon Prime Membership

Table of Contents

Introduction

I want to thank you and congratulate you for downloading the book Amazon Prime: How to Make the Most Out of the Many Benefits of Amazon Prime Membership. You are on your way to becoming a pro at using all the features Amazon Prime has to offer.

This book contains proven steps and strategies on how to truly make the most out of your Prime membership, including borrowing books, streaming media, and getting special member privileges such as fast, free shipping.

Here's an inescapable fact: there are so many benefits of a Prime membership, it is possible to be overwhelmed and not sure exactly what you can do with it. That is where this book comes in, providing an overview of benefits as well as some in-depth how-to instructions to really utilize Amazon Prime.

If you got your Prime membership just to use one feature, you may really miss out on other services that you would love. Amazon Prime is designed to make your life run smoother. You may find yourself surprised at some of the things Amazon Prime can do for you!

It's time for you to become an expert on using Amazon Prime and take advantage of the movies, television shows, music, photo storage, shopping options, books, and more available to you with your membership!

Chapter 1: Is Amazon Prime for Me?

Amazon Prime is not a free service, and you may be wondering if you will get enough use out of it to make it worth the $99/year or the $10.99/month. So what types of people will get the most use out of an Amazon Prime membership?

People who do a lot of online shopping can make their money back pretty quickly. You can shop for nearly anything on Amazon. True, any order of over $49 dollars made up of eligible items ships free even without Prime, but using standard shipping which can take 7-10 business days to arrive.

Prime members can have no minimum purchase when buying qualifying items in order to qualify for free 2-day shipping. If you frequently make smaller purchases or want free and fast shipping, you should consider becoming an Amazon Prime member,

Do you prefer watching television shows and movies through streaming services? Amazon has a large library and a comparable price to other services. When you throw in the other features you are getting as a member, Amazon Prime comes out looking like a better deal.

Amazon Video streaming is also available on most devices used by the other services. Amazon Video is the first to offer High Dynamic Range video quality, so if you are a stickler for the best in video and audio experience, an Amazon Prime membership could serve you well.

Want to stream music without interruptions? Amazon Music may not have as large of a library as some of the other streaming services, but as a Prime member, you will not have to listen to ads between songs or be limited to the number of times you can skip a track.

Are you a frequent flyer? If so, and you fly JetBlue, you can stream Prime music and videos for free on your flight. JetBlue has a fleet of Fly-Fi planes that allow you to access your Amazon Prime benefits. You can use your laptop, Android or iOS smartphone, or your Amazon Kindle to help the time and miles fly by.

Chapter 2: Overview of Benefits and Rules

Becoming an Amazon Prime member comes with a wide variety of benefits, as well as some rules and regulations you should be aware of. Let's talk about the perks first.

Shipping

Amazon Prime does not use one shipping carrier exclusively, but instead uses whichever one will get you your item in the time frame you have specified.

Many items on Amazon are available to receive free 2-day shipping in the continental United States. This applies to items sold by Amazon, not through the Amazon Marketplace. If you live in Hawaii, Alaska, or Puerto Rico, you will get free 3-7 day shipping instead.

It is important to note that the 2-day period starts after the item ships, so if you order something that is currently out of stock you will get it 2 days after they get the item in and ship it to you. Set your default shipping address to see reliable estimates of when your items will arrive. Remember, only business days count when calculating when your item will arrive.

Saturday shipping is available on some specially marked items, with prices starting at $7.99 and going up based on weight and size. Release-Date Delivery is an exciting and free shipping option available for qualifying items.

In some larger cities, Amazon Prime members can even get same-day shipping, as long as they select items marked eligible for the service. There is a minimum purchase of $35 for this service and orders generally have to be in by noon or they will be changed to free 1-day shipping.

This service is available 7 days a week, with the exception of major holidays and high volume shipping days, such as Black Friday. If you are not in a great hurry to get your items, you can choose No-Rush Shipping at check-out. If you do this,

Amazon will reward you with a promotional credit of some kind. The credit could be for music, videos, Amazon Pantry, or buying an e-book, among other things. You will be told what your specific credit is for when you choose your shipping method at checkout. You will still receive your item within 5 business days.

In order to hold on to your credit, do not cancel the No-Rush Shipping or return the item you ordered. Amazon will credit your account as soon as your order ships and even automatically apply it to qualifying purchases!

Prime Video

There are thousands of titles available to stream free for Prime members. Some titles are even available to download to an Amazon Kindle or mobile devices to view offline. The catalog of movies and T.V. shows changes frequently, so check back often to see what is new. There are also add-on video subscriptions available.

Prime Music

There are more than a million songs available to stream on compatible devices if you are an Amazon Prime member. This service is ad-free and available to those located within the United States and Puerto Rico. Playlists created by Amazon are available, and you have the option of custom making your own. You can even incorporate tracks you have to own your own computer.

Books

There are several advantages with your Amazon Prime membership involving downloading books. The Kindle Owner's Lending Library will be covered in detail in a later chapter. Members in the U.S. can also download one new book free per month earlier than non-members!

Shopping

In addition to the great shipping options, Amazon Prime opens up new options for what you can shop for and how. Whether you are shopping for electronics, clothes, birthday or Christmas gifts, or just stocking your pantry, Amazon has some exciting options for you. All the ways Amazon Prime can make shopping more fun and convenient will be covered later.

Prime Photos

Unlimited photo storage in the Amazon Cloud Drive is a major bonus of being a member. You will also receive 5 GB of storage for videos and documents. Photos are stored securely and can be backed up automatically if you choose. You can access your photos from anywhere. If photo storage is an issue for you, a Prime membership is actually cheaper than many external hard drives. If you do not renew or decide to cancel your membership, you will lose unlimited storage space and your photos will count towards your Amazon Drive storage limit.

The Rules

- Two-day shipping is not available for all items. Products not available for 2-day shipping will receive free standard shipping. These products generally have special shipping requirements.

- Amazon Prime is not intended for those who aim to resale their purchases made through Amazon.

- In some states, a sales tax will apply to your Amazon Prime Membership.

- Each specific feature of Amazon Prime will have its own rules and regulations specific to it.

Chapter 3: Membership Types and Sharing

Amazon Prime is the main and most common type of membership, and its benefits are what were discussed in the last chapter. You can either pay $99 for an entire year or pay $10.99 a month with the first month being considered a free trial either way. There are two variations of Prime memberships.

The first is Prime Student. In order to qualify for this type of membership, you will need to be currently enrolled in a college or university and have a valid .edu email address. With the student membership, there is no cost for the first six months, but you do not get all of the benefits of a standard membership.

You will still get the free 2-day shipping and access to thousands of streaming television shows and movies. If after six months you keep your account, you will be billed half the price of a non-student membership and get access to the full range of benefits.

There is also a Prime membership aimed at people only interested in video streaming. Prime Video memberships allow you to stream all of the videos available for Prime members.

It costs $8.99 a month, with no yearly-pay option. It does not come with any of the other benefits of a Prime membership, and it does not include any additional subscriptions, which you can still add.

Additionally, it is possible to get an Amazon Prime trial membership to see if using this service is right for you. When signing up for Prime, click *Start Your 30-Day Free Trial*. If you do not already have an Amazon account, you will be asked to make one now.

You will need to enter credit card information in order to get the trial. It is important to note that if you do not cancel after the 30-day period, you will be charged $99 for the year.

If you decide to cancel after the trial, log onto your account and click Settings. Then you will look for Manage Prime Account. On the left-hand side, there will be information on your trial account, including which day you will be charged for the year. Underneath this, you can click *Do Not Continue*. You will be asked to confirm this. After clicking this, all Prime benefits will stop unless you decide to buy a membership.

Membership Sharing

It is possible for up to two adults and four children to share one Amazon Prime membership. In order to do this, you must create an Amazon Household. Both adults need to be present to set this up.

You are able to link two separate Amazon accounts. Once both people are on the account, they can share many of the benefits of Amazon Prime as well as share content through a Family Library. You can share books, games, and apps this way.

Creating a household allows you to make profiles for your children and control the content they are viewing. Details on how to set Parental Controls for what your child can view can be found in the Prime Video chapter.

Kindle Freetime Unlimited

Another way to control what your child is viewing on Amazon when sharing your Prime account is to subscribe to Kindle Freetime Unlimited. This service does cost extra, but you receive a considerable discount when you are an Amazon Prime Member.

For one child, you will pay $2.99 a month instead of the $4.99 a month non-members pay. If you have more than one child, $6.99 allows you to have up to 4 child accounts, which beats the $9.99 non-members pay. This service is available on Kindle tablets, TVs, and Kindle readers.

In addition to blocking certain content, you can use this service to set educational goals and time limits. You can set it up so that your child cannot play games until their educational goals have been met for the day as well as let it know when bedtime is so that it shuts itself off. Kids do not have access to the internet or social media while using FreeTime and they cannot make in-app purchases.

It is a kid-friendly browsing environment that is ideal for children aged 3-12. Perhaps most importantly, kids cannot exit FreeTime without a password.

Giving Prime as a Gift

You can give the gift of a year of Amazon Prime to someone. In order to do this, provide Amazon with the gift recipient's email address and when you would like them to receive their gift. On this day, they will receive an email informing them of your gift and giving them instructions on how to activate their membership.

They can begin their membership right away. If they are already a member of Amazon Prime, they can exchange it for an Amazon.com gift card. The membership will not automatically renew after a year. Only a yearly membership is available for giving as a gift, and only the full Prime membership is an option.

If you happen to live in or plan to visit the Seattle area, there is a physical location for Amazon Books. You can purchase a Prime Card to give as a gift, which is redeemable for a full year of Prime membership.

Chapter 4: Reading with Prime

The Kindle Owners' Lending Library

One of the biggest perks when becoming an Amazon Prime member is the ability to check out one new book every month completely free. The Kindle Owners' Lending Library (KOLL) includes thousands of books, including over one hundred New York Times best sellers.

Borrowed books can be kept as long as you want but you may only have one out at a time. They can be read on Kindle e-readers as well as Kindle Fires and Fire phones as long as the device is registered to the account with the Prime membership. You can read your book on multiple devices as long as they are all linked to the same account. KOLL books cannot be read on the Kindle reading app.

To Borrow a Book

1. Open the Kindle Store on your compatible device.

2. Find the Kindle Owners' Lending Library on your device.

    a. On Kindle Fire tablets, select KOLL. On certain devices, you may need to swipe to the left in the Kindle Store to find KOLL.

    b. One Fire phones, swipe from the left inside the Kindle Store and then select *Kindle Lending Library*.

c. For Kindle e-readers, select either *All Categories* or *Menu* and find KOLL.

3. Choose a book. Eligible titles will have the Prime Badge underneath them.

4. Check out your book by hitting "Borrow for Free." If you still have last month's book, you will be prompted to return it at this time.

Please remember that if you cancel your membership or chose not to renew and have a borrowed KOLL book it will be automatically returned.

To Return a Book

1. Click on *Manage Your Devices and Content* and find the *Content* Tab.

2. Locate the book you would like to return and click the *Action* tab next to it.

3. Hit *Return This Book*. A dialogue box will come up asking if you are sure. Select yes.

Keep in mind there are no due dates. Any highlighting, bookmarking, or notes you have done will also be saved to your Amazon account, so if you decide to check out or buy the book in the future, you will still have them.

Kindle First

Do you like to be on top of the newest trends and hottest new book titles? If that is the case, Kindle First may make an Amazon Prime membership worth it all by itself. Each month, Amazon editors select six new books that are not available yet.

As a Prime member, you are entitled to select one of these books to read absolutely free each month, before their official release date. The books change each month and each month you are able to select a new book.

Kindle Unlimited

Kindle Unlimited IS NOT part of your Amazon Prime membership, but something you can subscribe to supplement it. If you are an avid reader and decide that you need more than two books a month (one from the KOLL and one through Kindle First,) you can subscribe to Kindle Unlimited. As the title implies, you can download an unlimited number of books that in are in the Kindle Unlimited library.

Keep in mind that large publishers generally do not allow their books to be included in this library and most books you can get using this service are at or below the $4.99 price point. Depending on what you read and how much you read, this may or may not be a useful addition to your Prime membership for you. It costs $9.99/month.

Borrowing Public Library Books

If you want the ability to read more books without paying extra, you can look into borrowing books from your local library. This is available to everyone, not just Amazon Prime members.

More than 11,000 libraries across the United States have partnered with Amazon to provide free book check-outs for Kindle.

You must be a member of the library you are trying to check a book out from. Using the specific library's website, you can check out Kindle books and have them sent to your Kindle Fire, Kindle e-reader, or your Kindle reading app. You will need to be connected to Wi-Fi while the library sends the book.

The service that offers this is called OverDrive. Which books are available, and the length you can keep them out will vary by library. When it is time for the book to go back,

Amazon will send you an email 3 days before it is due. You will also receive an email when the loan period is up, and the book has been returned. It is always possible to return a book before the loan period is up.

Chapter 5: Prime Instant Video

Streaming and downloading video is another big reason people get an Amazon Prime membership. Prime Video is only available to customers located in the United States and its territories due to licensing agreements.

The videos are available to watch on any compatible device through Amazon Video. Amazon Video can be used on your computer as well as the following devices: Fire phones, Fire sticks, smart TVs, Amazon Fire TVs, Blu-ray players, video game consoles (Wii, Playstation, Xbox,) Android and iOS devices (in the form of an app,) and set-top boxes (Roku, TiVo, Google TV.)

When searching for something to watch, look for the category *Prime Video* or *Included with Prime*. All these titles are viewable with no extra charge. You can also filter search results only to include those titles included with Prime.

Need another reason to consider getting Amazon Prime? Amazon has exclusive content, not available for streaming or downloading anywhere else. They also offer original programming, with many children's, comedy, and drama titles currently available and titles from all genres in the works.

First Episode Free allows you to watch the first episode of select TV seasons at no charge. This feature is available to anyone with an Amazon account. However, non-Prime members will have to sit through ad-breaks. To find eligible TV shows, open Amazon Video and find the *First Episode Free* category from either the *TV* or *Video* option.

Video quality will come at 4 different levels. They are Standard Definition (SD,) High Definition (HD,) and Ultra-High Definition (UHD.) What you are trying to watch and what device you are watching it on will affect which viewing options are available for you.

If Ultra-High Definition is not good enough, some titles are being released in High Dynamic Range (HDR.) You can only view titles in HDR if you are using the Amazon App on certain models of Samsung or Sony TVs.

Creating a Watchlist

Overwhelmed by all the titles you can now access? You can create a Watchlist so you can access the shows and movies you want to watch in the future in one convenient place.

This list is linked to both your account and your Amazon Video devices. When accessing it from the web, you can find *Your Watchlist* under *Your Account*. While browsing titles, you can simply click Add to Watchlist for things you think you will want to watch in the future. Already watched it or change your mind? Simply hit Remove from Watchlist under the video details.

Offline Viewing

Downloading certain titles to compatible devices is another option with membership. This is only available to the primary account holder; Household members receiving shared benefits are only eligible to stream video content. The devices that you can download content on are Kindle Fires that are newer than the 1st generation, Fire phones, and Android and iOS devices.

Each download will only be available for a specified time. This length of time varies by title. You will receive a notification when your downloaded content is about to expire. Prime Video is only available to customers in the United States and its territories.

To Download a Title

1. Ensure your device is connected to Wi-Fi. It will need to maintain this connection for the duration of the download.
2. Select the Prime title you wish to download and look for video details.
3. Hit download. If you are trying to download an episode of a television show, select the episode and then select download.

With Amazon Prime Video, you can also use Amazon's X-Ray feature. Amazon has partnered with the Internet Movie Database (IMDb) to provide information on actors, background information, and much more. This feature is not available for every title. Look for the *X-Ray* label on the details page.

The X-Ray feature is available while watching television shows or movies on your web browser, Android or iOS device, Fire tablet or TV, or Wii U. Whichever device you use, you will need to have access to Wi-Fi to use this feature.

Parental Controls

When using Amazon Video, especially when sharing with a household including young children, you may want to control what can be viewed and purchased. In order to do this, the first step is to set-up a 5-digit PIN. To set-up your PIN for the first time, access your account through your web browser or by using your Amazon Fire TV or TV stick.

After doing so, you will need to enter this PIN before you can make a purchase through Amazon Video. This does not apply to Amazon Fire devices (TV, tablet, or phone) because these already have built-in parental controls.

You can use this same PIN to set viewing restrictions based on rating categories. You can customize what ratings you would like restricted and on which devices this should apply. Amazon bases their ratings on the MPAA rating classification system for movies and the TV Guidelines Organization TV Parental Guidelines for television shows. They combined these ratings into viewing levels with recommended audiences. These levels are General, Family, Teen, and Mature.

The Amazon Fire TV and Amazon Fire TV Stick will also use the 5-digit PIN you use for Amazon Video. With these, you can make changes directly on your device. Open *Settings* from your Fire TV and select the *Parental Controls* option.

From here you can turn these controls on or off. It will ask you to enter your PIN or to set one up if you have not done so already. You can now block certain content and set viewing restrictions. You can also require the PIN to be entered to make any purchase, both digital and physical content.

There is a wide variety of controls you can set on your Amazon Fire Phone. To access them, go to *Settings*, *Applications*, and *Parental Controls*, then tap *Enable Parental Controls*. In addition to setting restrictions for video viewing, you can restrict social networking sharing, the camera, web browsing, internet access, and an assortment of other things.

The ability to restrict content on Kindle tablets depends on your type and generation. Once you have linked your tablet to your Amazon account, you can get personalized instructions for your specific device through their website.

Chapter 6: Prime Music

Amazon Prime members have access to millions of song titles. You can listen to music ad-free while enjoying unlimited skips. You can personalize a station based on your own music tastes. The list of songs available is always changing and worth checking often. You can also incorporate your own music from other sources into Amazon playlists.

The devices you can access Prime music on are as follows: Fire phones and tablets, the Amazon Fire TV, iOS and Android smartphones, Amazon Echo, the Fire TV stick, your PC or Mac, HEOS devices, Sonos devices, Play-Fi devices, and Bose SoundTouch systems.

The preferred format of music on Amazon in the Digital Music Store is MP3. Typically, 3-minute songs will take up approximately 5MB of space. Amazon also supports non-DMR files in .mp3 and .m4a for playback, streaming, and downloading. Eligible files formatted in .wav, .wma, .ogg, .aiff, and .flac files can be imported if Amazon has the rights to the track in their Digital Music Store.

If you have the downloaded Amazon Music app on your phone or tablet, you can download Prime music for offline enjoyment. This music is only available through the app and cannot be transferred to other devices. Once you have downloaded the music, switch from your *Cloud Library* to your *Offline Library*.

You can add music you own from other sources to your Amazon Music library. Go to *Your Music Library* from your web browser on the computer that contains the music you would like to add. *Upload Your Music* will be an option on the left-hand side. If you have not already, you will be prompted to download Amazon Music.

Follow the instructions on-screen. If you already have Amazon Music, you can skip the last two steps and open it directly. *Under Your Library* selects *Upload*. From here, you can drag and drop files into your music library.

Once you have done this, you can access this music from all of your connected Amazon Music devices. Add it to playlists to really customize your music experience.

While using Amazon Music, you can often view the song lyrics for the track you are listening to. This feature is available on Amazon Fire TVs and Tablets (except for the first generation Kindle Fire) and the Amazon App on Android and iOS devices. It can also be used through your web browser on either a PC or Mac.

If the song you are listening to has lyrics available, a Lyrics badge will appear next to the song title. On the Now Playing screen you will also see either *Lyrics* or *X-Ray* as an option. While listening to a song, lyrics will display line-by-line and in time with the playback in the lyrics panel.

This feature can be expanded to full screen or closed completely. If you are using a Kindle Fire

Tablet, you can press and hold a song to view its lyrics even if the song is not currently playing. Lyrics are available on songs you are streaming as well as for songs you have purchased through the Digital Music Store. You can match songs that you import to the Digital Music Store and view their lyrics as well. If the song was transferred using USB or is not currently in the Digital Music Store the song lyrics will be unavailable.

Some things to keep in mind about Amazon Prime Music are that it is only available to the primary account holder, not additional Household members, and that you must have a United States billing address. You must also have an Amazon account linked to a valid U.S. bank. This service is not available to those using the Amazon Prime Student membership during their trial period.

Chapter 7: Shopping with Prime

Amazon 1-Click

Amazon 1-Click allows you to skip the shopping cart and place orders with one click of a button. It is set-up automatically the first time you make a purchase on Amazon.

The method of payment and shipping address used for this first order will become your defaults for 1-Click shopping. It is important to keep this information up to date. Once you place an order, you have approximately 30 minutes to update your order information. You may turn off this option if you wish.

Amazon Prime Pantry

Prime Pantry is a service available exclusively to members, allowing you to purchase household goods at low prices and have them shipped at the low price of $5.99 per box. You can fit as much as possible in this box, which has a weight limit of 45 pounds and a size limit of 4 cubic feet.

You do not need to fill the box completely to make your order. Be sure to check out their weekly deals and exclusive coupons you qualify for by being a Prime member.

This service is aimed at people trying to restock their nonperishable household products. Some examples of things you may buy through this service are diapers, cans of soda pop, cat litter, canned foods, and pet food.

Having it delivered to your door for a low, flat rate can be much more convenient than a trip to the local bulk or grocery store. You can purchase both bulk and regular sized products through this service, adding to its appeal.

Exclusive Prime Coupons

There are many coupons available to Prime members exclusively. They are available for Grocery, Beauty Products, Health and Personal Care, School and Office Supplies, Automotive, and many other categories. On the coupon page, you will also see offers for Subscribe and Save.

If you order subscriptions, you will receive a discount on Amazon or Amazon Marketplace items you have subscribed for, and they will arrive on the same day every month. Shipping for this service is free.

You are not obligated to continue this service for any length of time and can cancel penalty free whenever suits you. You also have the option to skip a delivery if you are not ready for the next shipment. If you see a coupon you like, click *Clip Coupon* underneath the item, and the discount will be automatically applied at checkout.

Amazon Dash Button

An Amazon Dash Button allows the member to purchase buttons for popular products that you can then sync to your smartphone. Running out of an everyday item? Reordering can be as simple as pushing a button.

Once you receive the button or buttons you will be using; they must be linked to your Amazon account. Download the Amazon Shopping App from the Apple App Store or Google Play Store.

Turn on both Wi-Fi and Bluetooth on your smartphone. Some buttons do not use Bluetooth and will simply use the Wi-Fi and your phone's speakers to communicate. The next step is to open the Amazon Shopping App, select *Menu, Your Account, My Dash Devices*, and then *Set-Up a New Device*.

Sign in with your account and select *Accept and Get Started*. It is now time to hold down your Dash Button until the blue LED light flashes. In the app on your phone, hit Connect. You will then be prompted to enter your Wi-Fi network password. You can check the box to save the password, so you do not need to do this step every time.

Once the button is communicating with your phone, you will need to select exactly what product you want to be ordered when you click the button. This is where you can specify sizes and other variables.

For example, if you are re-ordering your laundry detergent, which scent do you want? You will do this through the app on your phone. Finally, you will be asked to confirm your 1-click shipping and payment information.

This is the info that will be used when you place an order. The final step is to find a convenient spot to stick the button. The button should be placed on a plastic or metal surface that has been cleaned in advance. In order to stick-on, remove the backing and hold down firmly for 10 seconds. To remove, slowly peel off. The best place for your button is a flat wall or another vertical surface.

Worried about accidental orders? When the button . is pressed, Amazon will send a confirmation notice to your phone. At this time, you can easily cancel the order if you change your mind, or it was unintentional. Unless you change this option, the Dash Button Order Protection will not allow a new order to be placed until the last order has been shipped.

Amazon Elements

The products available through Amazon Elements are designed to put the customer at ease because you know exactly what you are getting. They vow to listen to the feedback of the consumer when making all decisions regarding these products such as packaging design.

They will only use top of the line ingredients and things they are comfortable using with their own family. Being up-front about what you are buying, what is in the product, and how it is made is another way they hope to set you at ease. These products are available exclusively to Amazon Prime members.

Every Amazon Elements product comes with a code. This code can be scanned using your phone and the latest version of the Amazon App. While it looks similar, it is not a QR code, and you should not try to scan it using a QR scanner.

Peel off the top layer of the sticker and point your phone's camera at it to scan. The information that will pop-up includes when and where the product was made, its best-by date, when it was ordered, when it was delivered, the origin of each ingredient, the purpose of each ingredient, the story behind the suppliers, and other information specific to the product you have ordered.

It also gives you the opportunity to leave feedback and rate the product. Additionally, you can re-order the product using this code. If the sticker is missing, has been peeled off already, or is damaged in a way that prevents it from being scanned, Amazon cannot the origin and will either refund or replace your item.

Completion Discount

Amazon Prime can also help a family get ready for the arrival of a little one with 10-15% off of your online baby registry. Your registry will need to be at least 14 days old before you are eligible for this discount. You also need to be within 60 days of your due date.

When you have met the eligibility requirements, a message will appear on the top of your registry letting you know. The discount is good for an order up to 5000 US dollars, which will save you $750. You may use this discount one time only, up to 180 days after your due date.

To create your registry, click *Wish List* at the top of any Amazon.com page. Select *Baby Registry* from the drop-down menu that appears, then clicks *Create*. The on-screen instructions will walk you through the process of creating your new registry.

You can edit your name and email address in the *About You section*. You can also add a Co-Registrant so that people can search for the registry using your partner's name.

You can now search the Baby Store and other product categories and add things to your registry by clicking on Add to Baby Registry, located under the Buy button on the product's description page. You cannot add items that are currently out of stock on the registry.

Another baby-friendly benefit that Amazon offers is the diaper subscriptions, which can save you up to 20% and a trip to the store with a newborn.

Prime Now

Believe it or not, Prime customers in certain geographical areas can order items and food from restaurants and receive them in as little as an hour. This is a service available exclusively to Prime members, and it is available from 6 a.m. to midnight, 7 days a week. If you can wait two hours, the delivery is free. If you need it in an hour, the charge is $7.99.

There are tens of thousands of items available through this service, with more being added all of the time. When ordering from a restaurant, download the Prime Now app. If you live in an area that offers the service, you will see a selection of restaurants to choose from.

Once your order is placed, both the restaurant and delivery person are immediately notified. Amazon will then pick up the order and pack it in an insulated container and bring it to you. This should be done within the hour, with the average time being around 39 minutes.

Prime Day

This is a 1-day-only sale available exclusively to Amazon Prime members. Items go on sale from almost every product category, with some of the biggest discounts Amazon ever offers. These deals are comparable to prices you would find on Black Friday and happens once a year!

Video Game Discount

Are you or someone you love a big gamer? Amazon Prime members get 20% off pre-order and new release video games. This only applies to physical games (not digital downloads) that are shipped and sold by Amazon.

If you order during a game's pre-order period or within two weeks of its release, your 20% off discount will be automatically applied at checkout.

Lightning Deals and Prime Early Access

Special daily deals, called Lightning Deals, have a limited quantity available at a special discounted price. Anyone can shop for Lightning Deals, but certain deals have Prime Early Access which allows you to start shopping 30 minutes sooner than the general public.

Being a Prime member does not ensure you will get the deal as they are all "while supplies last" and some deals will sell out during the early access period. In addition to being limited in quantity available,

Lightning Deals are only available for a short period of time. You can browse future deals and place a Watch on upcoming deals to make sure you do not miss it. You will receive a notification on your phone if you have the latest version of the Amazon App and have notifications turned on.

Amazon Fresh

Amazon Fresh IS NOT included with Prime membership. However, Prime members can get a 90-day free trial of this service. The service is designed to offer early morning or next day delivery of fresh grocery products as well as things available to you locally.

Currently, only people living in Seattle, New York, or certain parts of California can use this service. Amazon hopes to expand it in the near future. If you decide you like the service after your 90-day trial period, it will cost you $299 a year to have both the Prime and Prime Fresh membership.

For such a steep price, what do you get? Amazon promises a high level of quality in the items you are receiving and takes extra care to keep things at their proper temperatures.

There are two options for when you receive your Fresh delivery. The first, and more popular, is Doorstep Delivery. With this option, you select a 3-hour window in which the package can be delivered.

You do not have to be home to receive the package, and it will come in a temperature-controlled tote bag. The bags are designed to keep your food fresh for up to one hour after the end of your delivery window. The totes are filled with frozen water bottles to keep your food cold.

These water bottles are safe to drink and do not need to be returned to Amazon. These tote-bags are collected when the driver drops off your next delivery. In order to qualify for Doorstep Delivery, the driver must have unobstructed access to your doorstep.

The other option you can choose is Attended Delivery. For this, you select a 1-hour window in which you promise to be home to receive your order. This is the option you will need to use if you live in a secure building. Another perk is you do not need to store their temperature-controlled tote bags in your home.

On top of paying to be a member, you will need to pay $7.99 for shipping if your order total is less than $35. Orders above that ship for free. Also, you will be required to cover the cost of the groceries you have ordered. Get your order in before 10 a.m. if you want to receive it the same day.

Additionally, if you do not wish to continue with Amazon Fresh after the trial period, it is up to you to cancel, or you will be automatically billed. The cost of the membership is pricey, but the items you buy can be significantly cheaper than you would find in stores so it may work out in your favor financially in the long run if you use the service a lot.

Chapter 8: Quick FAQs

- How much does it cost to join Amazon Prime?
  - A yearly membership costs $99, or you can pay $10.99 a month. A video-only membership is available at $8.99 a month. College students qualify for six months free and then a yearly membership at $49.
- How do you sign up for Amazon Prime?
  - Memberships can be purchased on Amazon.com. You will need an Amazon account and a valid credit card.
- Can you try Amazon Prime for free before buying?
  - A free trial of Amazon Prime is available if you have a valid credit card and Amazon account. Be sure to cancel before the 30-day trial period expires if you do not wish to be a member.
- How do I cancel my free trial?
  - Log into your account, click on *Manage Prime Membership* and click *Do Not Continue.*
- How do I cancel Amazon Prime if I am not in my free-trial period?
  - Log into your account, click on *Manage Prime Membership*, and select *End Membership.*
- What areas offer same-day shipping?

- This is available in Seattle/Tacoma, Los Angeles, the San Francisco area, San Diego, Fort Worth/Dallas, Phoenix, Indianapolis, New York City, Chicago, Baltimore, Atlanta, Tampa Bay, Washington DC, Orlando, Philadelphia, and Boston. Amazon hopes to continue expanding this service.
  - What areas offer Prime Now Restaurant delivery?
    - This service is currently available in Seattle, Dallas, Los Angeles, San Francisco, Atlanta, Austin, Miami, Baltimore, and Portland, OR. Amazon is expanding this service to other areas.
  - Do I get exclusive access to certain items?
    - Yes! On top of being able to shop Amazon's Element line, they occasionally offer items exclusively to Prime members.
  - What is an Amazon Household?
    - Amazon Households are created to share digital content and certain Prime benefits with other members of your family. You can add two adults, each with a separate Amazon account, and up to four children to your Amazon Household.
  - What benefits can be shared with members of my Amazon Household?

- The benefits that can be shared are as follows: Streaming Prime Video, the fast and free Prime shipping options, early access to Amazon Lightning Deals, the benefits of Prime Photos (each adult has their own unlimited account and will not share actual photos or albums,) use of the Kindle Owners' Lending Library, the 20% off diaper subscription discount, and the 15% discount on their baby registry.
  - What is Prime Day?
    - Prime Day is a member-only sales event, where Amazon promises discounts and deals to rival the ones usually reserved for Black Friday, all from the comfort of your own home.
  - Where can I watch Amazon Prime Videos?
    - Almost any device is now compatible with Amazon Prime. You can watch on PCs, Macs, the newest generations of all gaming systems, Kindle tablets, as well as many Smart TVs and smartphones. Unless you previously downloaded the title, you will need internet access.
  - Is will being a Prime member give me access to all of Amazon Video's titles for free?
    - No, it will not. Not all titles are available under Prime and those

that are not will need to be
purchased separately.
- Do I need to be online to access Prime
  Video and Music?
  - For the most part, Amazon Music
    and Amazon Video are streaming
    services. However, as a Prime
    member, you can download
    certain titles so that you can
    enjoy them even if your device is
    offline.
- What items generally qualify for 2-day
  shipping?
  - Almost all items sold by Amazon
    will qualify. Larger items, like
    treadmills and other oversized
    items, may not. Those sold by
    third parties via the Amazon
    Marketplace may not; it is up to
    the individual seller.
- Does Amazon offer a referral credit for
  people who get family and friends to
  sign up?
  - Yes, they do. If the person you
    refer is a first-time Prime
    member, you will receive a $10
    credit the first time an order they
    placed after becoming
    memberships. If the person
    recently had a free-trial, they may
    not qualify to earn you the referral
    credit. This credit is not available
    to people living in Arkansas,
    Colorado, Maine, Missouri,
    Rhode Island, and Vermont due
    to restrictions in those states.

- There is also a credit for referring someone to a Student Prime membership. This credit is for $5, and there is no purchase necessary to receive your credit. Both you and your friend will receive the credit, though it may take up to 7 days to show up in your account.
  - Does Amazon Prime come with Kindle Freetime Unlimited?
    - No, it does not. It is an optional addition that you can purchase for a discount if you are a Prime member.

Conclusion

Thank you again for downloading this book!

I hope this book was able to help you to make the very most out of your Amazon Prime membership.

The next step is to start using Amazon to do the things you love, whether it be listening to music, reading a good book, watching the latest television shows and movies, storing your photos or doing some online shopping. Simplify your life with fast and free shipping on everyday products and easy product ordering.

Finally, if you enjoyed this book, please take the time to share your thoughts and post a review on Amazon. It'd be greatly appreciated!

Thank you and good luck!

www.ingramcontent.com/pod-product-compliance
Lightning Source LLC
Chambersburg PA
CBHW06020529052 6
45789CB00003B/1162